How To Draw
CATS

Written and Illustrated
by **Janet Rancan**

Watermill Press

10 9 8 7 6 5

materials

The first thing you'll need to draw the cats in this book is some white paper. It doesn't matter what kind, but make sure it's big enough.

You might find tracing paper helpful. You can trace over the first three steps of each picture until you feel that you can do it on your own.

An eraser is good to have just in case you make a mistake.

You should have a couple of sharpened No. 2 pencils. They are good for drawing the first three steps of your picture. Keep your beginning pencil lines very light and you won't have to erase them.

You can do your finished drawing in a very soft lead drawing pencil. Or, you can use colored pencils.

Here are some ways to draw the different kinds of fur on the cats in this book.

Short, smooth fur. Use light strokes that are very close together. Press lightly, or use the side of your pencil.

Spots and stripes. Keep the edges soft and jagged, not hard and stiff.

Long silky hair. Draw long, flowing lines. Don't make them straight, or you'll wind up with a porcupine.

Fluffy fur. Draw short, light strokes that are slightly curved. Leave a little space between the hairs.

use simple shapes

All things are made up of simple shapes—circles, triangles, ovals. If you start with these shapes, drawing the cats in this book will be easy and fun.

You might find it helpful to trace the first three steps. Then, fill in the details on your own. Little by little, your drawing will begin to take shape.

Don't try to do too much too soon. Keep your pencil lines light. This way if you make a mistake, it'll be easy to erase.

Here is the finished picture. You can add color to make it more lifelike. Remember, start out slowly by drawing simple shapes. After a while, you may be able to eliminate one or two of the steps. Don't get discouraged if your drawings look different from the pictures in this book. Each of us has our own personal way of working. Just relax and have fun developing your own style of drawing.

draw the head of a cat

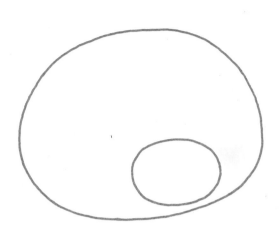

Take a good look at a cat. Notice that the head is made up of circles. First, draw a big circle. Then, put a smaller circle inside of it.

Add two little circles for the eyes. Draw two ears, a nose, and a mouth. It's already starting to look like a cat!

Now you can start to fill in some details. Give the cat slanted eyes and a real nose. When you complete this step, you will be ready to finish your drawing.

Make your cat look real by filling in some details around the eyes. Draw in some fur and don't forget the whiskers!

draw the head of a kitten

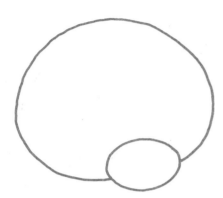

A kitten has a large head with large ears, but a tiny face. Draw a big circle for the head. Inside the circle, put a smaller circle.

Draw two large triangles on top for the ears. Add a small triangle for the nose. Give the kitten two eyes and a mouth.

Once you've done your basic shapes, you can start to add some details. Draw the inside of the ears and give the kitten a chin.

Kittens are full of curiosity, so make its eyes big and wide. Turn the mouth into a little smile. Compare the cat and the kitten. Can you see how they are different?

draw a cat

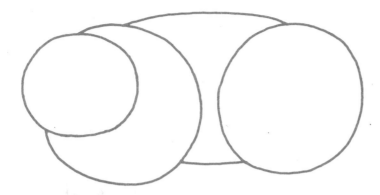

Here is a cat for you to draw. Start your drawing with the basic shapes of the head and body. Draw a circle for the head. Then a larger circle for the shoulders and one for the hips or hindquarters. Connect the shoulders to the hips by drawing a line on the top for the backbone and a line on the bottom for the stomach. This basic step will be used to draw all of the cats in this book.

Give the cat two front legs attached to the shoulders and two rear legs attached to the hips. Add a tail. Don't forget to start the face, but keep it simple.

Erase some of the basic shape guidelines that you used to form the cat's body in Step 1. Give the feet some shape by adding toes.

The pupils in a cat's eyes are not round, like a person's, but they work exactly the same way. In bright light, they appear as vertical slits. In dim light, they widen to let more light into the eye.

Finish your cat by coloring in the eyes and the fur. This cat looks just about ready to go on the prowl.

draw a striped cat

Start your drawing very simply by making three circles—one on top of the other, like a snowman.

Give the cat a face by drawing in some basic shapes. Add legs, feet, and a tail.

Give the cat some toes and slanted eyes. You can erase some of your beginning lines now.

Now color your cat and give it some stripes. Make sure the fur looks soft—not hard and stiff.

draw a little kitten

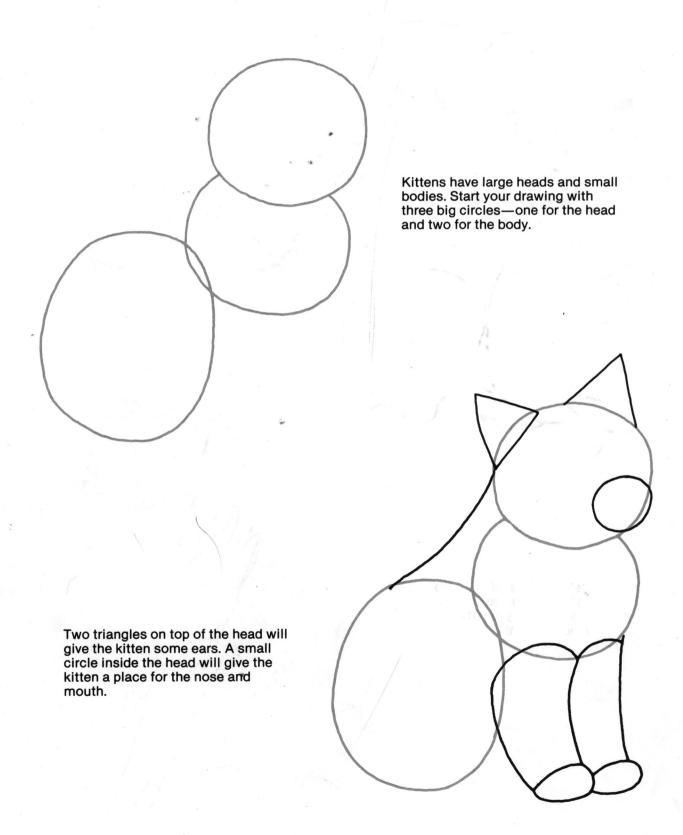

Kittens have large heads and small bodies. Start your drawing with three big circles—one for the head and two for the body.

Two triangles on top of the head will give the kitten some ears. A small circle inside the head will give the kitten a place for the nose and mouth.

Draw in a face—give this kitten large eyes, a tiny nose, and a mouth. Then, draw the feet and a little tail.

Kitten fur is very soft and fluffy, so don't make it look too heavy. Big round eyes will make your kitten look cute and innocent.

draw a playful kitten

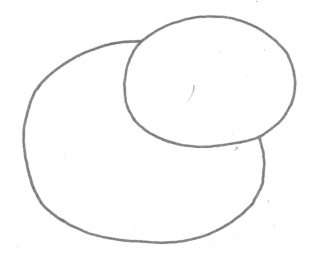

Little kittens have lots of energy. This kitten is ready for some fun. Start with big round shapes for the head and body.

Now add legs for your kitten to run on. Animals use their tails for balance. Draw this kitten's tail straight up in the air. Add ears and a circle where the nose and mouth will go.

Remember, a kitten's face is small. If you make it too big, it will look more like a cat than a kitten.

Kitten fur is soft and fluffy. Start out lightly and fill in your dark colors last.

This kitten is now ready to play. Try drawing some more kittens to play with this one.

draw a Persian Cat

Persian cats originally came from Asia. Their luxurious coats can grow up to 5″ (12 centimeters) long. These cats require a lot of brushing and special care to keep them looking well groomed. Persians have short legs and stocky bodies. They are bred in a variety of colors.

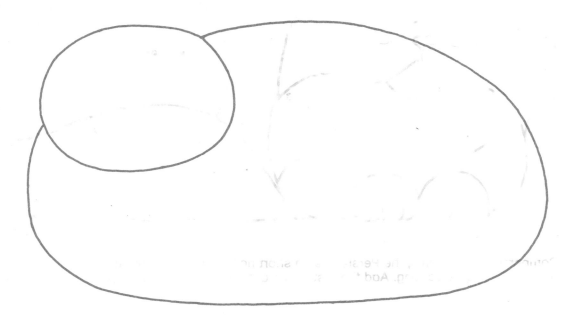

Start this Persian cat by drawing two ovals—one for the head and one for the body.

Persians have small ears, so don't make them too big. Give this cat a big, bushy tail. Add the eyes, two front paws, and an oval where the nose and mouth will go.

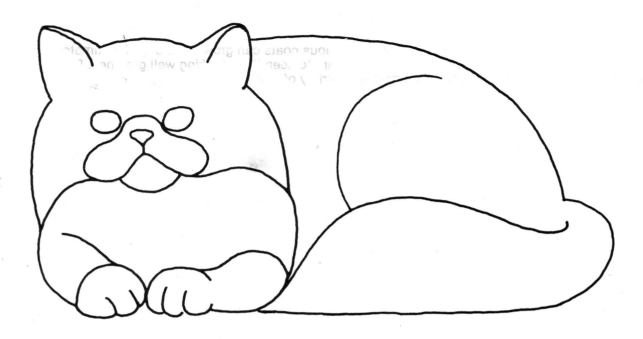

Compared to other cats, the Persian has a short nose. Its jowls look big because the fur is so long. Add the rest of the details.

Persian cats are calmer and quieter than other cats. They prefer to lounge around the house rather than look for adventures outside.

draw a Siamese Cat

The Siamese was the royal cat of the kingdom of Siam, which is now called Thailand. This popular cat is known for its blue eyes, its loud voice, and its wedge-shaped head. Kittens look almost white at birth, but as they mature, their head, legs, and tail darken. These dark areas are called "points." There are four varieties of Siamese cats: the seal point, the chocolate point, the lilac point, and the blue point.

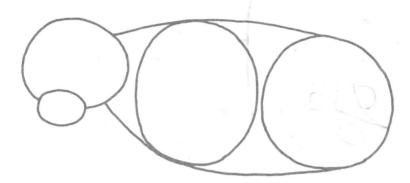

Draw a circle for the head, and a smaller circle at the bottom for the mouth. For the body, draw two circles—one for the shoulders and one for the hips. Connect top and bottom.

Start adding the "points"—the legs, tail, ears, and face.

Siamese cats are very active and are good hunters. Their bodies are usually slim and sleek.

The Siamese has short fur. Its body is usually tan with brown or blackish-brown points. The blue and the lilac point Siamese are a bluish-gray color.

draw a Himalayan Cat

The Himalayan is a cross between the Siamese and the Persian. This cat has the chunky body, short legs, and long wavy coat of the Persian, with the markings and coloring of the Siamese. Himalayan cats have blue eyes.

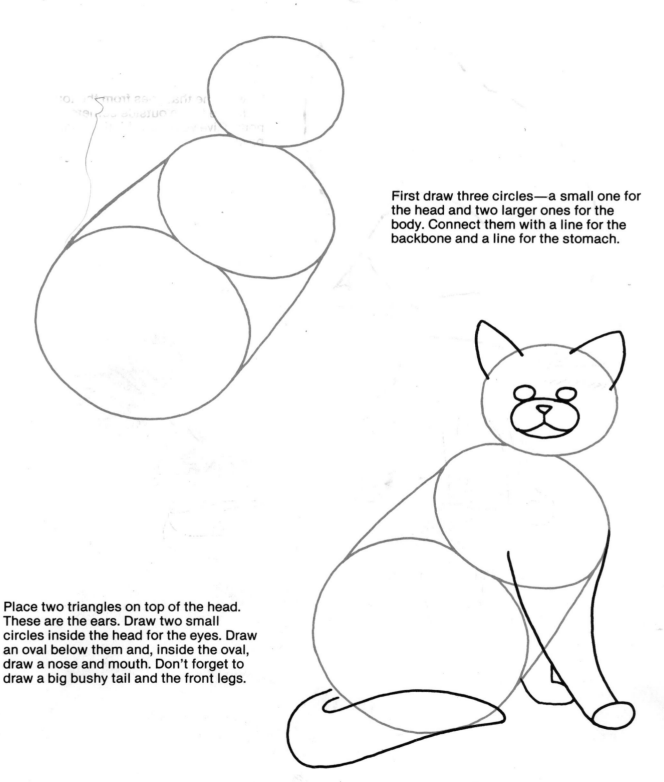

First draw three circles—a small one for the head and two larger ones for the body. Connect them with a line for the backbone and a line for the stomach.

Place two triangles on top of the head. These are the ears. Draw two small circles inside the head for the eyes. Draw an oval below them and, inside the oval, draw a nose and mouth. Don't forget to draw a big bushy tail and the front legs.

Draw a line that goes from the top of each eye to the outside corners of the nose. Give your cat a hind leg and some paws.

Now you can draw in the fur. Remember, the Himalayan has dark points like a Siamese. That means the ears, the face, the lower legs, and the tail are darker than the body.

draw a Manx Cat

The Manx cat comes from the Isle of Man, an island between England and Ireland. The true Manx do not have tails and are known as "rumpies." They have thick, double coats and long hind legs. They walk with a rabbit-like hop.

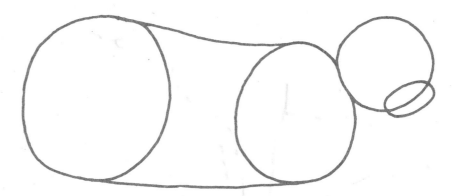

Start this tailless cat by drawing the head and body. Add long hind legs and shorter front legs. Because the hind legs are longer than the front legs, the top of the hindquarters will be almost as high as the top of the head. Now draw the rest of the details.

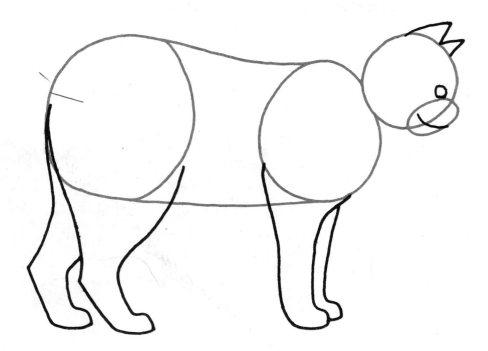

Another variety of Manx cat has a short stump for a tail. These cats are called "stumpies." However, the "rumpies"—the ones with no tails at all—are considered the only true breed. Do not draw a tail on this cat.

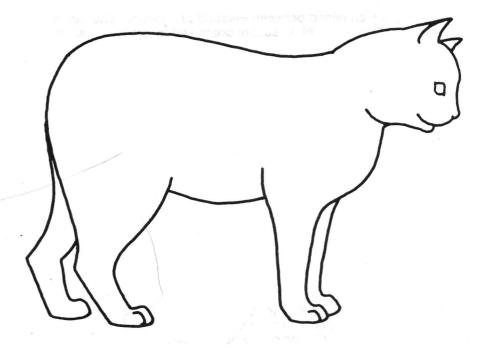

According to legend, the Manx lost its tail while going aboard Noah's Ark. The cat tried slipping through just as Noah shut the door, cutting off its tail.

draw an Abyssinian Cat

The Abyssinian is known for its long ears, small head, and slender body. Its fur is "ticked." This means that each hair is marked with several different colors, starting out silvery near the skin, and gradually changing to brown and then to black.

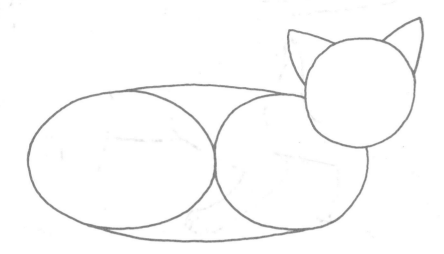

Draw a head and body. Give this cat long ears.

Abyssinians have long, graceful legs. Their feet are small. They enjoy swimming and, at one time, were trained to retrieve water birds for hunters.

The Abyssinian has almond-shaped eyes that are either green, yellow, or hazel. The tip of its tail and the pads on its feet are black.

draw a tiger

The fierce tiger is well known for its beautiful tawny coat and its bold, black stripes. The orange and black pattern forms a perfect camouflage in the dark shadows of the jungle.

Draw a big circle that's flat on the bottom. Inside the circle, draw an oval.

Inside the oval draw a triangle for the nose. Below the triangle, draw a mouth. Draw two small circles for the eyes. On top of the head, place two half-circles. These will become the ears.

Draw a line across the top of each eye to the tip of the nose. Also draw two lines that go all the way around the inside of the face—from one side of the mouth to the other.

Draw some stripes across the top of the head, around the eyes, and down the sides of the face. Outline the eyes in black and give the nose some nostrils.

When drawing stripes, remember: tigers are covered with hair. The stripes are just bands of dark hair arranged next to bands of light hair.

The tiger has white patches of fur around the eyes, around the mouth, and down the sides of the face. The rest of the face is a tawny yellow color and the stripes are black. No two tigers are marked exactly the same way.

draw a lion

At one time, lions roamed throughout much of Europe, Asia, and Africa. Today, wild lions inhabit only parts of Africa and northern India. The adult male can weigh as much as 400 pounds (180 kilograms). His long mane grows across his head, shoulders, and chest. The female is smaller than the male, and she does not have a mane.

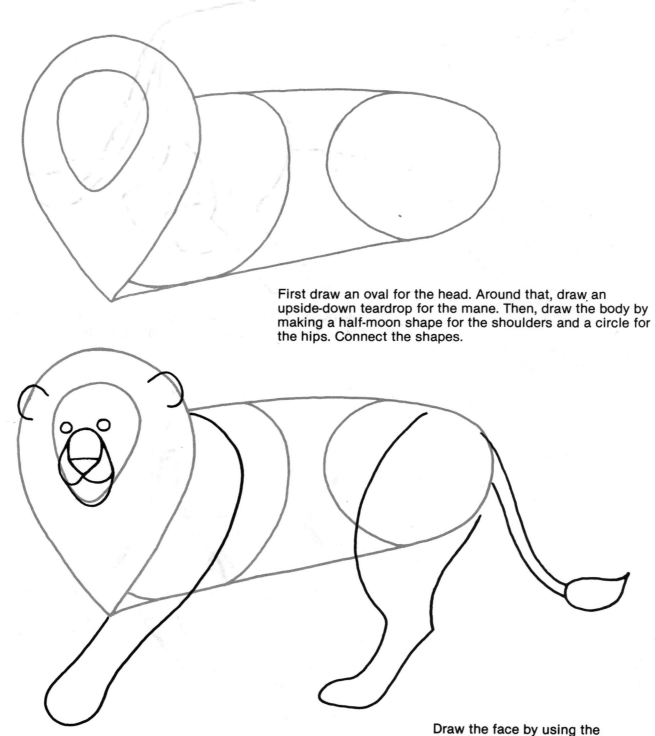

First draw an oval for the head. Around that, draw an upside-down teardrop for the mane. Then, draw the body by making a half-moon shape for the shoulders and a circle for the hips. Connect the shapes.

Draw the face by using the same shapes that you used on the other cats. Place ears on the top of the mane. Draw two legs and a tail.

Add details to the face and draw in the other two legs. This lion is now ready for your own finishing touches.

The lion's regal appearance has earned him the title, "King of the Jungle."

draw a jaguar

The jaguar is native to the Western Hemisphere. This cat resembles the leopard but is larger and much heavier. It is also marked a little differently. The jaguar's spots, called "rosettes," have small spots inside.

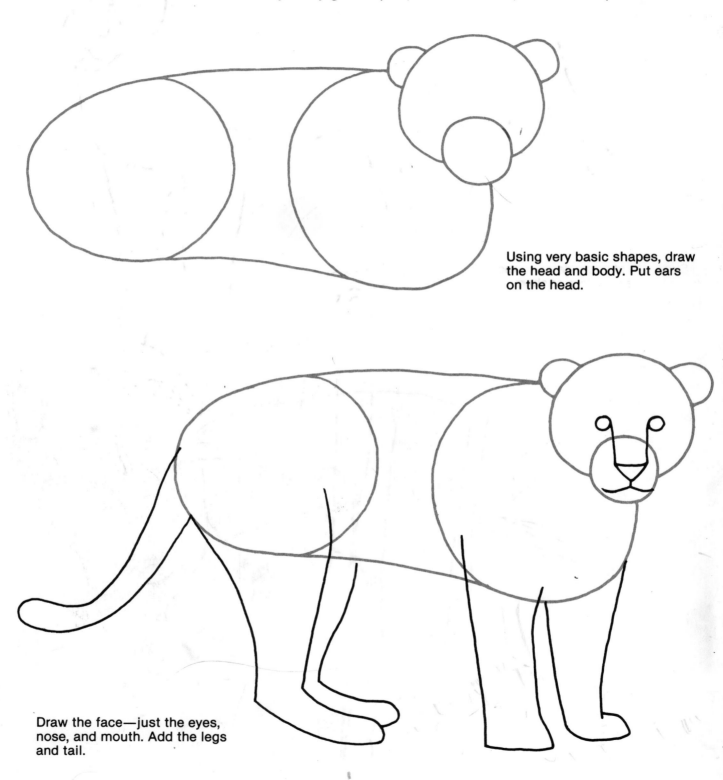

Using very basic shapes, draw the head and body. Put ears on the head.

Draw the face—just the eyes, nose, and mouth. Add the legs and tail.

Start to add some detail to the face. Give your jaguar sharp eyes.

The jaguar's spots are solid black dots. They appear around the face, the tail, and the lower outside legs. The spots turn into stripes on the inside of the legs.

draw a bobcat

The bobcat, also called the "American Wildcat," is the only wild cat native to North America. It can be found as far north as southern Canada and as far south as the tip of Mexico. The bobcat is the size of a large house cat. It has a spotted reddish-brown coat, black tufted ears, and a short stubby tail. Its striped face is surrounded with long sideburns.

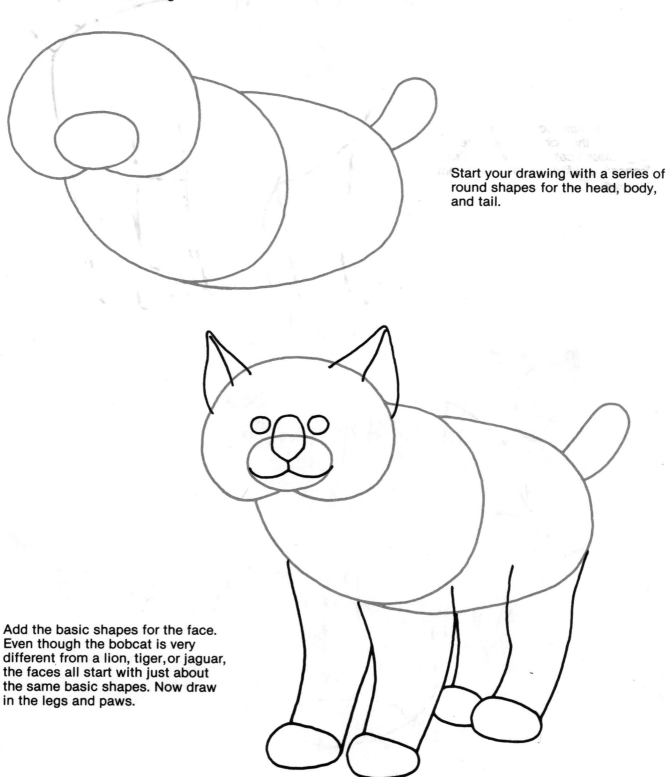

Start your drawing with a series of round shapes for the head, body, and tail.

Add the basic shapes for the face. Even though the bobcat is very different from a lion, tiger, or jaguar, the faces all start with just about the same basic shapes. Now draw in the legs and paws.

Make the face more catlike. Although the bobcat looks like a large house cat, it is a wild animal. Bobcats are fighters and excellent hunters.

The bobcat is mostly reddish-brown, but the belly and the chest are white. There is also some white on the face and on the underside of the tail.

This book covers only a few different kinds of cats. There are many other breeds, both domestic and wild. All cats, big and small, belong to the same cat family. Next time you see a cat, take a good look. Try to see the basic shapes of the head and the body. Whether you're drawing a house cat or a jungle cat, the basic shapes remain the same. If you can draw these simple shapes, you can draw any cat you choose.